Changing Shape

by Donna Foley

PEARSON

Scott
Foresman

DK

What You Already Know

Matter is anything that takes up space and has mass. Matter can be a solid, liquid, or gas. Solids have their own shapes. They do not change shape when they move. Liquids can change shape. They take the shapes of their containers. Gases can change shape and size. Air is a gas.

Matter can change in many ways. Different kinds of matter can mix. Some solids can dissolve in liquids. This means that the solid can spread throughout the liquid. Some liquids can evaporate. Evaporate means to change from a liquid to a gas.

Sugar dissolves in hot drinks.

Matter can change from one kind to another. Sometimes the change is forever. Sometimes matter can change back and forth. Water is a liquid. It can change. Water freezes when it gets very cold. It is then ice. Heat melts ice. Ice changes to water when it gets warm. Water boils when it gets hot. It changes to a gas. This gas is water vapor. You cannot see water vapor.

In this book you will learn about ways that other kinds of matter change shape.

Matter and Shape

Different kinds of matter can take different shapes. Solids keep their own shapes. Each block has a size and shape that does not change. Link them together. They can make a new shape. But each block stays the same shape.

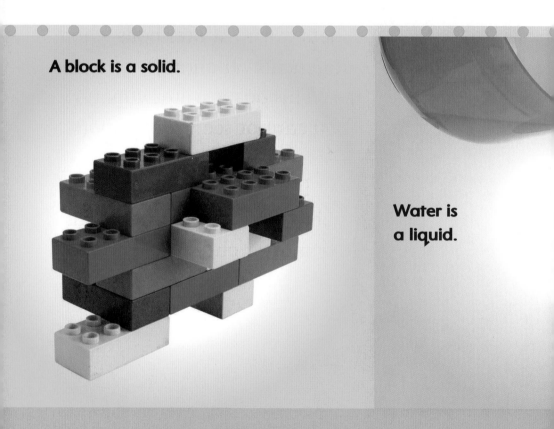

A block is a solid.

Water is a liquid.

Liquids are different from solids. They take the shapes of their containers. First the water takes the shape of the jug. Pour it into a glass. Now it takes the shape of the glass.

Gases are different from liquids and solids. They take the shapes of their containers, like liquids. But they can change size too.

Air in the ball is a gas.

Change It

Force can change the shape of matter. Force is a push or pull that moves or changes matter. The hammer hits the candy with force. The candy breaks into little pieces. The force of the hammer changes the shape of the candy. Do you think the hammer has to hit it with a lot of force?

If you stretch a balloon, the shape will change. If you let it go, the shape will change back.

Balloons can stretch. Your hands pull the balloon. This makes a force. The balloon changes shape. When you let go, it goes back to the shape it was.

Clay can change shape too. You can bend, pull, and push it to make new shapes.

Twist and Bend It

A sponge is matter. It is a solid. It is soft. You can squeeze it. You can twist and bend it. You can change its shape. It is twisted up inside the cup. When you take it out, it goes back to the shape it was.

The shape of the sponge changes.

8

Balloons are solids filled with air! Air is a gas. Balloons change shape when you twist or bend them. The air inside the balloon moves around. Then the balloon takes a new shape. It can take the shape of a hat. It can take the shape of an animal too!

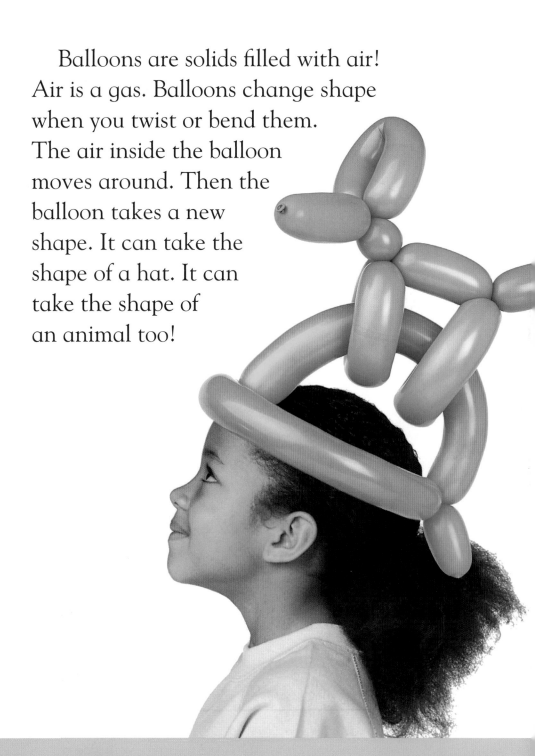

Stretch It

The chef is making noodles. Noodles can stretch before they are cooked. They change their shape when you pull them. Look how long and thin they can get.

The noodle dough can stretch a lot!

Some people wear suspenders. Suspenders help keep pants up. Suspenders can stretch. They change shape when you pull them. But they will change back when you let go of them.

Roll and Squash It

You can shape clay again and again. It is soft and will not break. You can use the force of your hands to change it.

Blacksmiths need to heat metal so they can shape it.

Metal is a very hard solid. But it can change shape too. Some adults have jobs where they need to change the shape of metal to make new things. They use fire to make the metal very hot. Then they use a hammer and other tools to bang and shape it. It takes a lot of force to change the shape of metal.

Melt and Cool It

Candles are made of wax. Wax can change shape too. The flame makes heat. The heat melts the wax. It changes from a solid to a liquid. The wax cools after it drips down the candle. Then it changes into a solid again!

Matter can change shape in many ways. Different kinds of force make this happen. What other ways can you think of to use force to change the shape of matter?

Glossary

force   a push or a pull that moves or changes something

hammer   a tool you use to hit something

metal   a hard material that is usually shiny

noodles   a food made of flour and water, and sometimes milk or eggs

squash   to press until something is flat

squeeze   to push or press hard against something

stretch   to make something longer